HA HA HA HAA!

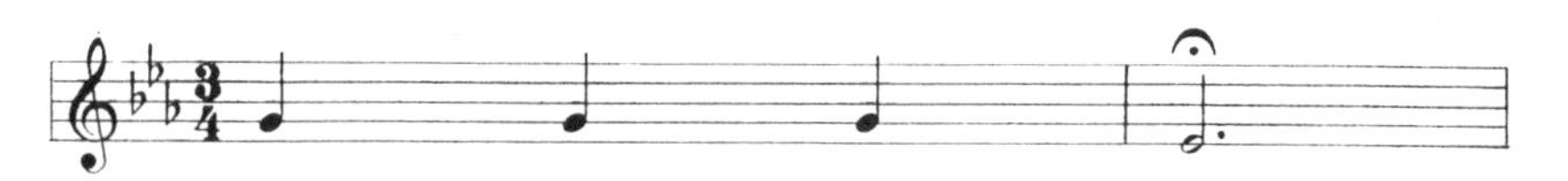

Quips, Quotes and Cartoons for Music Lovers

by

Joel Rothman

For Marion

I Play a musical instrument a little,
but only for my own amazement.
Fred Allen

First published in Great Britain in 2000 by Robson Books,
10 Blenheim Court, Brewery Road, London N7 9NT

A member of the Chrysalis Group plc

British Library Cataloguing in Publication Data
A catalogue record for this title is available from the British Library

ISBN 1 86105 363 0

Printed in Great Britain by Creative Print and Design (Wales),
Eddw Vale

If you want to learn an instrument, try the piano — then you'll have somewhere to rest your drink.

UPRIGHT PIANO —
an instrument that can be downright annoying.

Practice makes perfect — nuisances!

Such a considerate boy —
always wore gloves when he practiced piano
so he wouldn't disturb the neighbours.

Your son has a great ear for music!

Do you know the scale?
Sure — It's 50 bucks for sidemen and double for leader!

Einstein, the great mathematician, enjoyed practicing his violin, and he often played duets with his friend Arhur Schnabel. One day as they were playing at Schnabel's house, Einstein began to have difficulty coordinating a particular passage with the piano part. "My dear Albert," asked Schnabel, "What is the problem? Can't you count?"

Dear Sir:
Your pianos are the best I've ever leaned on.
Will Rogers

Ma — I just got married!
"That's nice. Did you practice your piano today?"
Oscar Levant

VIOLINISTS —
People who are always up to their chin in music.

To learn the violin you must first begin from scratch.

Stop practicing that violin — your'e driving me crazy!
But dad — I stopped two hours ago!
Dad has hidden my violin. Doesn't anyone here like music?

The musician said, "I told your reviewer that I was playing on a genuine Stradivarius, and he didn't mention a word about it in his review." The editor replied "That's exactly how it should be. If Mr Stradivarius is to have his products mentioned in this paper, he'll have to go about it like everyone else and pay for an advertisement."

One of his relatives claimed that Jack Benny had the only Stradivarius made in Japan.

If it isn't a Stradivarius I've been robbed of 35 bucks!

Jack Benny

I've always wanted to be a double bass player but I can't make the height requirement!

Tell the truth, Harry — is there someone else?

ROTHMAN SCHOOL OF MUSIC
You mean I hitched my way across the country to enroll in this school and the course finished yesterday
SCOTLAND

PERFECTIONIST —
A musician who feels the need to complete things from A to G.

HARP —
A piano in the nude.

UNCARING HARPISTS —
Musicians who just dont give a pluck.

Remember — playing harp in this world won't qualify you for playing harp in the next.

HEAVEN —
A place that's overmanned in the string section.

The famous band leader, Tommy Dorsey, was being interviewed. He was asked "In all your years of playing what was the most frequent request?" He answered straight-away, "Where's the mens room?"

SLIDE TROMBONE —
The phallic instrument of the orchestra.

CHILD PRODIGY —
Usually a kid with highly imaginative parents.

I can only suggest that you play the slide on your trombone with your left hand!
DOCTOR

TUBA PLAYER —
Someone who has to say
"Excuse me" after every note.

A musician got mad at his wife for putting his saxophone and violin on top of their T.V. set. He told her, "There's enough sax and violins on television!"

Wow — just once in a lifetime you hit a note like that!

I don't see how we can move him on — he's playing the national anthem.

The first thing a child learns after he gets his first drum is that he's never going to get another one.

If you don't stop playing those bloody drums I'll go mad!
BANG! BANG!
BANG!
Thank God you were on the gig, Joel.
BASS DRUM

What did you learn at your first drum lesson?
Not enough — I have to go back again next week!

Does my little girl have a talent for the drums?
About as much as the Venus de Milo!

My drum teacher shot himself during the lesson!

Mom says I can only stay for three hours.

Does it ever occur to you why we're so unpopular in this building?

Those jungle drummers really swing!
BOOM!
BOOM!
BOOM!
BOOM!

You're screwin' up the music, man. When I booked you you said you could read drum parts at sight.
I can - but not at first sight.
What do you think of the drummer we just auditioned?
He can't keep time — but that's his only fault.

I didn't know you play the drums, Fred.
I don't — I bought them off the kid next door.

I've made my contribution to cleaning up the pollution.
SKIP

A wealthy man had one longing ambition — to be a conductor. So one day he hired an entire orchestra to rehearse them. He knew virtually nothing about conducting, and his incompetance annoyed the musicians so much that at one point the timpanist sent up a cresendo roll to a resounding triple forte. However, it was played about thirty measures too soon, during a passage that was supposed to be pianissimo. The man conducting became so furious that he threw down his baton and shouted, "Okay, who was the wise-guy that did that?"

I think you should take a rest and forget all about the timpani for a while.

A percussionist was asked,
"What do you have to know
to play cymbals?"
"Nothing," was the reply. "Just when."

XYLOPHONE —

an instrument for converting timber into timbre.

I heard a sad but not uncommon story of a young boy who fell in love with something 36-24-36. It was his guitar!

Yesterday I played an old Benny Goodman album for my ten-year-old son. "That was one of the hottest groups back in the forties," I said. He listened closely and found it hard to believe. He asked, "You mean with only one guitar?"

FAMOUS MUSICIAN —
A person who works hard all his life to become well-known, then wears dark glasses to avoid being recognized.

COUNTRY MUSIC — Pop corn. (It's often thought of as rural music sung by ear through the nose.)

FOLK SINGER —

Someone who sings about the simple life using a $10,000 sound system.

"How did you get that big bump on your head?"
"The audience threw tomatoes at me last night."
"But tomatoes are soft"
"Not when they're in cans!"

TONE DEAF —
A somewhat misleading expression, especially when you listen to certain singers — you'd swear they were *stone* deaf.

Rock music has changed one thing —
the world may no longer end with
a bang — but with a twang!

The rock groups today bring a fantastic amount of electrical equipment to their gigs. I know one musician who gets paid for doubling — he plays lead guitar and fuse box.

I've never heard such corny lyrics, such whimpering sentimentality, such repetitious uninspired melody. Man we've got a hit on our hands!

Those rock lyrics he writes are for the ages — ages three to five!

I could eat alphabet soup and shit better lyrics than that!

Johnny Mercer

When I hear some of today's rock music I think to myself, if Vincent Van Gogh was still alive he'd probably cut off both ears!

Such a wonderful young band — they have hearts of gold, wills of steel, and ears of tin!

MUSIC MANAGER —

Someone who becomes aggravated at the idea that some crummy rock group can command 90% of his salary.

One famous musician left instructions which read: "After I die please have my body cremated, and send ten percent of the ashes to my agent."

Now I'd like to give my impression of a rock star singing his latest hit. First, I whack my thumb hard with a hammer!

ROCK DYNAMICS —
Loud, louder, deafening!

During one drought-ridden summer a teenage girl asked her grandfather to take her to a live rock concert being held in the town square. At the concert the lead singer was screamin' and shoutin' and putting his body through all sorts of gyrations. When the concert ended the teenager turned to her grandfather and asked, "How'd ya like it Gramps?" "I'll be damned, girl," replied the old man, "If that don't bring rain, nothin' will."

PUNK ROCK —
Audible grime - the highest form of noise. (It's a sound that burst upon the music scene like a ripe boil.)

PUNK ROCKERS —

Kids who dress alike, eat alike, talk alike, think alike, look alike — and what are they against? Conformity!

We're the world's ugliest band. When we play I expect to find puke in the aisles.
Bob Colemby
(Blood, Sweat and Tears)

It's a noise we make, that's all. You can be nice and call it music.
Mick Jagger.

This is no exaggeration — there's one rock performer who sings so badly that deaf people refuse to watch his lips move!

How can those rock cats afford all that sound gear they use?
Well — just think of all the money they must've saved on music lessons!
HEAVY ROCK CONCERT
TONIGHT
TWISTED METAL · AXEHEAD · INCINERATOR · SKULL DEATH

The one thing that reassures me about contemporary rock is the thought that things just can't be as bad as they sound.

Atheists are really on the spot. They have to sing, "Hmmmmm Bless America."

A famous rock star was autographing copies of his new album. One man walked up to him and said, "My wife loves your songs, so I thought I'd give her a signed copy of your latest recording for her birthday."
"It's a surprise for her, eh?" asked the rock star.
"I'll say," agreed the man "She's expecting a new car."

Great news for people who hate rock music — they've developed a compact disc that spins twice as fast. It doesn't sound better but it's over quicker!

DANCE FLOOR —
A place where some people love to dance while others dance to love.

TANGO —
The vertical expression of a horizontal idea — a form of floorplay.

She may not dance well but boy can she intermission!

JAZZ HIT PARADE — Top of the bops.

Did you hear about the American D.J. who kept referring to Australia as being on the flip side of the earth?

BOP —
The kind of music that no matter what you play comes out all right.

Hal Jackson.

Playing bop is like playing scrabble with all the vowels missing.

Duke Ellington

My grandfather was an old dixieland jazz musician, my father played swing music, and I'm a modern jazz musician. My son probably won't work either.

If you haven't had a gig for three years why don't you try something else?
I can't, man — it's my living!

I know one overweight jazz musician whose only concept of exercise is snapping his fingers on two and four.

But dad, I'm really happy playing piano with a progressive jazz group.
Listen to him Hilda — ten years of classical training and all he's got to show for it is happiness.

He was Jewish she was black and the love of his life. Seeing her lying on the bed he was filled with desire. Lifting her long slim body, he placed his lips directly over her mouth. She cried out in a soft mellow voice — their moods were perfectly in tune. Benny Goodman and his clarinet.

BLUES SINGER —
Someone who can make every day sound like Yom Kippur.
Lionel Hampton

SCATTING —
A style of singing by jazz vocalists who live in constant fear that they might remember the words.

CONDUCTOR —
A person who should never get ulcers — he should give them!

On matters of intonation and technicalities I am more than a martinet — I am a martinetissimo.

Leopold Stokowski.

Why do we in England engage at our concerts so many third rate continental conductors when we have so many second-rate ones of our own?

Sir Thomas Beecham

As an orchestral conductor he didn't know his brass from his oboe.

BROADWAY —
Where they sell cut-rate tickets for flop shows and cut-throat tickets for hit ones.

The new musical was a big success — the audience was a failure.

At the end of the performance Groucho Marx said to the producer "I've had a wonderful evening - this wasn't it!"

The producer asked the conductor, "What do you think of the acoustics in this new thatre?" "Splendid," he replied , "you can hear every cough."

CHORUS GIRL —
A woman who's determined to show her musical ability or bust.

TAPE MEASURE —
An instrument that's sometines used to judge the musical ability of a show girl.

NUDE MUSICAL —
An extravaganza in which the cast barely makes a living. For the producer it's a risqué business.

I saw a nude show the other night. All the chorus girls were running round in tight fitting costumes — skin!

Singing is every mans' bathright.

If you must sing, do it in the shower — the sound of running water is a great help.

The first Sunday I sang in a church choir
two hundred people changed their religion.

Fred Allen

When I'm sad I sing, then others can be sad with me.

Fred Allen

A little Mexican boy was told to write the first stanza of The Star Spangled Banner, so he began: "Jose can you see?"

After teaching my second graders 'America The Beautiful' I listened while they sang it for me. And one voice rang out above the rest — "Oh Beautiful, for space-ship skies..."

Marilyn Kilby

She has a singular voice —
thank god it isn't plural.

When she said "I'm yours
for a song," I didn't realize
she meant the Wedding March!

You'd better take two — my wife is about to sing!

Poor dear — it's her first professional performance — she must have an authentic case of stage fright!

A young composer of opera who had written two arias, invited the great Rossini to listen to them and say which one he preferred. The young composer was playing the first aria when Rossini interrupted and said, "You need not play any more — I prefer the other."

People are wrong when they say opera isn't what it used to be. It *is* what it used to be. That's what's wrong with it.

Noel Coward

Enrico Caruso was known to be one of the most active lovers of his time. It's claimed he once said, "I never make love in the morning — it's bad for the voice, it's bad for health and, besides, you never know who you might meet in the afternoon."

They spent a million on this production — and that was just to reinforce the stage!

I like Wagners' music better than anybody's;
It is so loud one can talk the whole time
without other people hearing what you say.

Oscar Wilde

OPERETTA —
Someone who works for
a telephone company.

After the tenor's performance the audience shouted, "Fine! Fine!", and before the poor guy was allowed to go home he actually had to pay it.

As Sir Thomas Beecham was conducting a rather uninspired production of Aida, a horse that was on stage began to defecate while the tenor was singing. Beecham whispered to his first violinist, "Just look at that - the horse has turned critic."

When the critic was asked how he could sleep through the opera, he replied, "Sleep is a form of criticism."

MUSICAL PLAGIARIST —
A composer who gives birth to an adopted child.

It's been said that Handel often lifted ideas from other composers without feeling in the least bit guilty. In one of his operas over 100 measures were stolen from a minor composer. When confronted with this fact he said. "That's true, but it was much too good for him."

CHAMBER MUSIC — A conversation between friends. (With some groups it sounds like it's coming from a torture chamber!)

Brief review in a local newspaper:
"An amateur chamber group appeared at the recital hall last night to play Brahms. Brahms lost."

Oh well, you play Bach your way. I'll play him his.

Wanda Landowska,

harpsichordist, to fellow musician.

Beethoven once told a fellow composer,
"I liked your opera. I think I'll set it to music."

Having adapted Beethoven's Sixth Symphony for 'Fantasia', Walt Disney is reported to have commented, "Gee, this will make Beethoven."

GOOD COMPOSER —
A person who never imitates -he steals!
Stravinsky

His music used to be original. Now it's aboriginal.
Ernest Newman
on Stravinsky